GLIMMERGLASS GIRL

poems by

Holly Lyn Walrath

Finishing Line Press
Georgetown, Kentucky

GLIMMERGLASS GIRL

for Gregory,
who never put me behind glass

This is a work of fiction. Names, characters, incidents, and places are
either products of the authors imagination or used fictitiously. Any
resemblance to actual events or locales or persons, living or dead, is
entirely coincidental.

Publisher: Leah Maines
Editor: Christen Kincaid
Cover Art: © 2018 Geoff Gallice
Author Photo: Holly Lyn Walrath
Cover Design: Holly Lyn Walrath

Printed in the USA on acid-free paper.
Order online: www.finishinglinepress.com
          also available on amazon.com

Author inquiries and mail orders:
Finishing Line Press
P. O. Box 1626
Georgetown, Kentucky 40324
U. S. A.

Table of Contents

On Womanhood

This chapbook is a fantastical account of womanhood. It draws upon my personal experience; however, I acknowledge with a whole heart that this experience is not that of every woman, nor is it the experience of everyone who identifies as a woman. My Glimmerglass Girl is merely a shadow of myself, so I ask only that you hold her gently, for she may slip away before you have come to fully know her.

Espejitos

in the night glass is everywhere / making the concrete a
river / dusting the filth with nymph sweat / so as to
rarify the mist / mirroring dashboard altars / hiding in
storefronts / echoing in gutters / glass is dangerous /
glass is invisible / glass is dirty /

fluttering amidst the stars / stands the thin black stalk /
of a glimmerglass girl /

her maker made her to disappear / dim / fade away /
outline / to paraphrase / herself /

catch her—catcher—scoop her up in your hand /

grasp the thin chitin / of her butterfly wings / like
holding onto the surface of water / between two
fingerprints / between your teeth / rub away her scales /
with the heat of your skin /

but before you imprint yourself / on the thin of her
wings / remember the question / unasked / yes or no? /

burn it into your retinas / tattoo it on your cheeks / tuck
it into your manly smile / learn how to ask / so that she
can say no / you may be unfamiliar with this answer /
no /

but remember the properties of glass / or her ghost may
follow you in the mirrors / forever / in store windows /
forever / in the glint of your razor blade / no / forever
/ no /

Self Portrait through an iPhone

At first glance is surprise—is this what I look like to him—eyes down-shot—drifting left to right—the act of self-interrogation—and yet what redeems me to you—female recompenses mean nothing—the twinge of hair burned red by the sun—the lips on which fine lines of aging make deeper, harder—the smoothness of cheeks still pink with sylphen shock—in the background hangs a version of you—a younger interpretation—so little changes since the act of self-love—blackening her eyes—bruising her lips like throwing an apple at a wall—these things seem natural—but I still don't recognize you like I should—I still don't know how to love you like myself.

Peony Red

Looking out over the overgrown yard
through the light of the kitchen window

she plunges her hands into
the soapy water—oranges.

The feathering suds on the tension
surface—little delirious delicacies.

Her hands are soft and diminishing,
becoming like the petals of the peony
or lace paper—gold leaf.

Outside—neighborhood children
walk in the tree line over the river.

The one little one—a china plate
impossibly tender white face
with low blue eyes rolling
on it like bright coat buttons.

If she were to touch that bending
head—peony red—oh what then?

Yesterday, kneeling in the stone-
walled garden, toes in the mud,
she shaved each bud and saved
the roots of the red bouquet.

Today, hours after the sin,
the peony tea consumed,
the deed done and easily,
the boy dead in the water.

Housewife

I am peeling the crisp brown suits
off of a pair of onions, reproving
for the clock is digging in
between the ribs and marinade,
it hates the night time sour.

I am broken over the boiling vinegar
and sweet-faced green cucumbers,
knobbed and vulgar, peeled away
to meet their maker.

The house—four rooms with bows tied
end to end to counterfeit the confidence of it
concealed behind draperies
that hemorrhage orange daybreak
onto end tables, side tables, console tables.

Pouring out the one beam
like hot lemon meringue filling
in the blinds, I see it as a slanted scowl,
sad thing, keeping out the
bright, keeping me in, custodian.

In Rejoice of Kindred Grief

girl in blue
lacy torn dress
backless denuded bra
struggling against two lavish breasts
clear hanger straps crestfallen
zipper half-zipped no one to zip her up
mouse-brown roots of dyed blue hair
voice stretching up and up until it cracks
mood ring cobalt with sadness like one more
tomorrow to get through and she talks
plainly of hope in a way only she can pray
he will hear empyrean guilt tinging her words
but he turns his beer bottle sideways
grasping at the door handle with claws
the next blossom drowns in waiting
for a blue rapture blessing—for anyone to truly
see her drunken starlight as female beauty
for a body that's not a four-letter word
for one true kiss

Behind the Glass

Reproduction
as you put it
is biological.
Superior and necessary,
those were the words you used
as the red wine seeped
up to our eyeballs and
spilled out onto my cheeks.

Behind our words we
shored up a house of crystal,
knocking us about in its hollow heart.

(The ocean breeze tried to tear it up
with its teeth but it stands like a stalwart
old sailor, shipwrecked after his last voyage,
head rimmed with hoarfrost, clinging
to the salt-soaked rocks.)

We live in a world
of unfulfilled fairytales.

You were promised
I would be dainty
with a size three foot
(to fit the glass slipper),
a bell dangling in my skirts,
an apron bow like a present,
and flowers on my knees
(red, blushing violently).

I was promised you would be tall,
spritely, piney-handed (handy)
golden-curled (sweat-soaked tendriled)
wearing a coat with three buttons
ruffled feathers beneath, a popinjay—
with a sugar-dusted tongue
and after I tasted you—

Yes,
promises we made
behind the glass.

Two Young Wives

We two sat
on the swing
on the porch
in the house
by Range Lake.

We talked about
the future, which
seemed to end in May.

There—in May—a threshold.
A bridge between our old lives,
where we were pillars
striving to be wood, strong,
to hold up.
Where we were young,
before thirty rose up
and devoured us,
showing its face
at first in secret places
blue starburst veins,
dimpled smile lines.

Cupping hot cups
of blueberry coffee
we watched yellow oak
and brown pine
and red maple
leaves falling.
They never seemed
to reach the ground,
drifting out over the lake
whose surface was pinched
as if by some invisible touch.

And you remarked,
"I see now how a seed
could be spread across the ocean."

Elegy for a Body

I take up ashes
like taking up space.
I am dis-embodying my body
or what I once called skin,
its remnants rounding out,
the insides of a funeral urn
whose curves make sense.

Inside here with me
the afreet's ghost
and the memory of feeling thin
like a butterfly's wing
like water in a glass pitcher
like telephone wires
filled with energy
of the me I remember only
in the soft nail beds
and crane's neck
and boy's chest
of yesterday.

She Learns How to Disappear

She memorizes little spaces she could hide in—
the white place between letters on the page
the dashboard radio like a golden dais
the corner of the yard where crows suckle
the cherry streetlight which creates the rain
the empyrean sky with its open space
where she could be a splinter in the expanse
fold up like an origami swan
tuck her face under her wing, blasphemed.
This one thing is clear—she knows
one more day is purgatory.

Woman

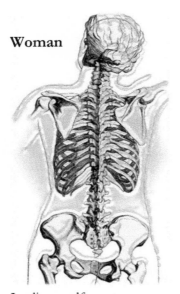

I split myself apart
parting seas
seaward bound prow
prowling wood hewn rough
rough as the chill of
children bored and head shaven
shave skin and iris from pupil
pills white as I go under
undertaker pulling down my slip
slipping between me and slivers
silver knives like butter
bitter African cocoa flour
flower on my tongue fleeting
floats away in the dark in
darkness I am both fire
firebrand and ice cleft in sunlight
asunder from the horizon's earth
earth and sky black and white hoary year
yearling shorn
sworn I am bating
baited I am woman.

Wind-Up Girl

if you open her box / she unfolds at her ankles / and sound wavers out of her prison / her eyes wander / the mirror radiates nuclear emissions / blue casts her in a favorable light / for her skin is impossible porcelain / filling the sink of her skin / faking radiation in her cheeks / she imagines the feel of his hand in hers / the warm, almost damp center / of his palm like a world / revolving slowly in it / she is held / he watches her turn / music softly tinkling / and her head tilted just so— he can hold her hands up like / ballerinas dance / like a kissing prayer.

Anvil Crawler

I am night and a thousand stars hurtle through
my skin, punching through the ether.
I crouch, prehistoric, in the space behind clouds, my volcanic heart
attracting lightning, sympathetic
interstellar.

My shadow is a supernova cutting a path through the light,
slimming ever thinner until nothing else remains.
My insides negative, the darkness turned out,
pepper-black and coal-hard.

Lightning waits for me on the other side of the forest.
He's tall and thin, pale or blue, holding me in
but this isn't a cage. These aren't flowers I'm pollenating—
they're caves spelunked, mountains cliff-hung, open seas hard to
port, hives honey-brimmed and buzzing places where
I can hide.

Morning Song

I have drawn a
face on the paper and
while she is not
human she is not quite
dead either which is
to say that maybe she
is not real or maybe
she is coming for me as I curl
into the lumpy throw.
I can hear the train
feebly in the distance
its tracks run across the
green of my neighborhood
you can hear it in the
yard with the fat brown
birds jabbing.
What do they see in
the dirt
something and the cats
squished all higgly-piggly
in the window tails
flicking side to
side like the clock
my grandfather wound every night.
Train whistles at the stop
soft sleep noises
from you and I thought
why must
you be awake now when
I am just getting
my engine going?

Aerie

Our bones hollow fingertips into feather
pinions tinged with gold.
We hide in silver linings quills
line down cotton scrapbook
nests, sinews mold the quiet mess
of a body of light—the light of a body.
We soar into flare—burn brighter.
Burn a hole with a lighter
and view us in it.

The walls built of sheaves
of words cleaved from books
penned by a sister's hand
tiny and sweet serif finite
sand poured over dead dry ink.

We remnants of light like sunbeam
hoops, petals pressed into walls
like men's mouths, men who pick
up our light, pop it in lick
greasy fingers, brush our snow
small and precious off their
charcoal suits.

I Want to be a Grackle, I Want to Caw

In the winter when the trees are raw, you can see bird nests, which in any other season would be cloaked, secreted away behind one great screen of jade, safe.

The nests roost between naked limbs, which themselves look like one great nest made by some giant bird, perhaps a wren or sparrow, yet sadly fragmentary, as if some hand pinched the bird away to place it in a cage.

The nests float, it seems that they should fall, that it is incredible that they might be held up by only the tantalizing knotting made by a bird's small yellow beak. They shudder, they vacillate in the air, top-heavy.

How do the birds feel when the leaves start to fall? Do they miss the sweet isolation, the privacy from a predator's eyes, the feel of vegetation sentient around them?

I once lived in an apartment fringed with trees. When the leaves fell, I could suddenly see into my neighbor's windows. I closed my curtains.

Sometimes I feel dense, like my head might break away, drift into the firmament like a child's lost balloon, red and shiny. I feel like the winter bird nest, top-heavy. I shiver, I long to conceal, I draw the veil.

Two Hundred Fifty-Seven

I have eaten 142 sunflower seeds today
(roasted, unsalted, in-shell) and written
257 words across a blank piece of paper, today
I told the character in the science fiction novel
he will die, and he responded with the casual
and unbroken flick of a middle finger
between his top and bottom teeth, today
I imagined several haikus that could
not really be defined as such but
at least they looked pretty, in a nice
little block shape like literary wood
engravings on sheepskin or the desperate
secret note of a fugitive, squeezed
onto the back of a postage stamp, today
I revisited the scene in the back
of the black pickup with the blood
on the floorboards, concealed by the
litter of cigarette butts, coins and receipts
and reckless cell phones that will
not stop ringing hip hop ringtones, today
the pregnant girl, wooed by the stack
of gold rings upon the older man's
fingers, will not escape into the thick
crowd of New York bodies and mist
that lies at their feet like death's
odor, she will not deface her
rapist, branding him for the bastard
he is with the hush of a gun, today
I could not solve the world's
problems so instead of beginning anew
I made honey lemon herbal tea, which
was so hot that I had to drop a tiny
ice cube onto its surface, which refused
to melt away anyway, but at least today

I managed to recreate the sound
between my teeth when my pursed lips
hit my tongue and the cat comes running
besides which the noise of perfect
silence.

Blue Cadillac

Oh, the way you sat in
the drive, taking it all up.

I climbed into your cool interior, sliding
across the widest, darkest navy seats
spread beyond me, beyond my vision.
They seemed to expand and dissolve
into a bright light on the driver's side.

We drove, through endless lanes
of white picket fences, long green,
green lawns, the Texas sun staccato
in the trees, and it may be that I wore
an Easter Sunday dress, all laced in white,
and bows on my tights, or white slumping socks
above black buckle shoes shining with polish.

And in the heat of a Texas summer,
how you could swallow me up
in your blue dusty smell, that
sweet sweet tobacco tucked
into the glove compartment
beside a lady's silver lighter.
For the sun merely seemed
to enclose you, a line of gold
light above the leather dash.

But the very roundness of you, round seats
and silver knobs and panels like porthole
windows into another time, but mostly
the round, stitched-leather steering wheel
which was surely made for white driving gloves.

And somehow in this memory of you,
your massive lines like some primordial
behemoth long since dead and buried in
ice, the very blueness of you, I may have
remembered myself, another classic beauty.

The Art of Loneliness

I tell my sisters:
cultivate loneliness
like you might care for
an orchid, turning it
gently towards the light,
serving it water like wine
aerated, purified, filtered.

This may mean
learning to eat alone without
someone to order for you,
or choose your wine, or share
a plate. You may learn
to eat an entire serving
alone, at peace, smugly.

This may mean
learning to watch a movie
alone, no one to hold
your hand, or interject
with a kiss, or whisper
in your ear. You may learn
to guard peace, taking in each
word, moment, image.

This may mean
learning to live alone without
anyone to cook for, or clean up after,
or hold close at night
in darkness. You may learn
to sleep through the night,
warmed by the thought of
your own existence.

In all its
exquisite shuddering beauty
loneliness can fester, wounded,
and eat up your heart,
leaving only a dark grotto,
etched with predators.

Give loneliness its due time
letting it blossom out
until it becomes unruly.
Then reign it back in.

Premise of the Heart

My heart is a flat horizon, a flush, rugged
coastline peppered with refineries and silt,
smog, and fire, littered with bodies, netted
redfish, kings, and sharks.

  Yet, for once my heart does not
  decay, does not sputter hot oil and turmoil,
  coastal storms. No, it is glass-thin, translucent,
  mosaic, stained calm at sunrise reflecting light.

    Despite, my heart wants for pain. I suspect
    it may never trust me again, expecting me to
    squander its beauty, pin it up in weird places like a
    glittering beetle—green-winged and blind, to taste
    its copper backbone like a mouthful of nails—
    heartless.

Heart as Seen through Camera Obscura

I find myself constantly surprised by the viciousness
of my own blistered heart.
Given the chance to be gentle, to be generous,
I will inevitably kill the ginger.

But my own cruelty belies even my own desires
  to be pleasant—supplicant—giving. Selfish, I encircle myself. I
barb wire. I, tantamount to nothing, am incapable of

love—except possibly the biting, melting kind that asking, refuses
return.

But this gives me power. It makes me fierce.
We will not give in. We will not see ourselves through this smallest
of pinholes.

We will look upon ourselves,
whole and blinding.

I am Going to Find the Unicorns
After Edward Hirsch

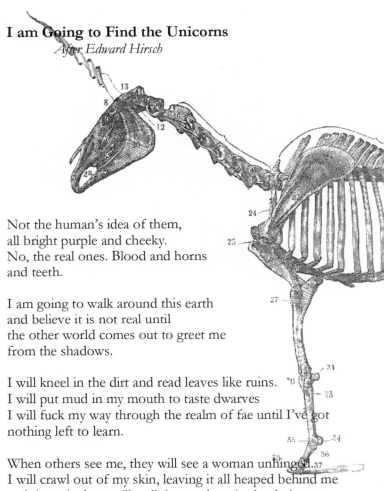

Not the human's idea of them,
all bright purple and cheeky.
No, the real ones. Blood and horns
and teeth.

I am going to walk around this earth
and believe it is not real until
the other world comes out to greet me
from the shadows.

I will kneel in the dirt and read leaves like ruins.
I will put mud in my mouth to taste dwarves
I will fuck my way through the realm of fae until I've got
nothing left to learn.

When others see me, they will see a woman unhinged.
I will crawl out of my skin, leaving it all heaped behind me
and the naked me will walk home alone in the darkness
a disciple of shadows, an acolyte of the moon.

When the unicorns find me, I will learn to fight
even when there's nothing left to fight for.

I Swallowed the Moon

It wasn't just that I swallowed the moon in all its entirety, the craggy surface that so many times I looked up to during my life, making faces out of the dark surfaces and when it waned imagining it like a slice of pie which needed eating, its round shape haunting drawings I made in art class, its glow a suggestion of another world outside the blinds over my window at night,

but that in eating it whole, without biting my teeth down on it like a crumbling chocolate square, feeling its heavy body slip down my gullet, seeing my stomach at once pregnant with its round shape, I knew I doomed the world, tideless, with my appetite.

I Think My Taste is Questionable

In my childhood, I ate one ninety-nine cent candy bar a day,
walking home from the gas station,
a cold Dr. Pepper between my legs to unlock
the gate behind the woods. I had a panache
for Smarties, hoarded at Halloween,
and I would slowly bite their white rims
until a hard heart remained.

In my teens, ahead of my time, I drank Jello shots
that gulped down, formed a strange pile
like Gummy Bears at the bottom of my self-respect.
At the movies I ordered tubs of popcorn
and Sour Patch Kids, and sat in the back row with my friends
dreaming about the projectionist and his freckles.

In my twenties, I smoked clove cigarettes
coiled in brown paper, little love letters
chased them with orange Sour Altoids,
which at first glittered with a layer of diamond white dust
but later, in the hot car on a Texas day
congealed into sticky-sweet oblivion.

In my thirties, I developed a taste for pickles
and sunflower seeds, the latter's shrouds littering
my desk, in the cracks of the couch and my bra,
the former folded in white paper, saved for later,
always in secret, to avoid uncomfortable questions.

Will I take up pig's feet in my forties? Perhaps
kimchi and caviar? Will I finally mature a taste
for Grape Nuts, like my father? Or will I swill
a Diet Coke with brunch like my mother?
Or perhaps, the tawny suicide
of a Jameson bottle close
at hand, under my pillow
like a tooth for my
guardian fairy?
Like my brother?

White Matter

He pulls down my jeans and underwear in one swift motion.

Is it raining?

He kisses the butter-soft left cheek of my bottom.

Or do I kiss him?

I stand, hands gripping the yellow wheel of a playscape pirate ship which is crumbling with rust, his lips pressed against my cold skin.

Or is it him?

Four years younger, blue-eyed, blond hair crushed like the hay we hunted needles in, and I kneeling before him, my knees wet on the wood.

Or was it a field?

I wish this memory into dream. If I dream it enough, it frays thin, dies a ghost death easier than his, the boy I played with on a wet fall day.

Or was it summer?

I am normal. I have a little boy with brown hair. He plays with Legos, makes mountains of them, flying machines, spaceships. I watch him closely, looking, waiting.

Acknowledgements

Images used in this book are a part of the public domain, PD-US, and have been adapted by the author for this work, or are used by permission of the artist.

"AD57, Nymphalidae, Ithomiinae, Ithomia sp," by Geoff Gallice.

"Glass Wing Butterfly Panama," by Dirk van der Made.

"A Peony," by Wenceslaus Hollar, Wenceslaus Hollar Digital Collection, Thomas Fisher Rare Book Library, University of Toronto.

"Alice au pays des merveilles," *Alice's Adventures in Wonderland*, illustrated by John Tenniel, 1865.

"Seeds and Leaves," from *The Forest Nursery: Collection of Tree Seeds and Propagation of Seedlings*, by George B. Sudworth, 1900.

"Woman holding water jug," from *Fairy Tales of India*, 1892, Illustrated by John Dickson Batten.

"Gibson Girl," Charles Dana Gibson, 1891.

"Skeleton Woman Back," Dr. Julius Kollmann, 1910.

"Ballerina," by Rudy and Peter Skitterians.

"Nest of Song-Thrush" from *Natural History, Birds*, illustrated by Philip Henry Gosse, 1849.

"Birds Illustrated Eggs," from *Birds Illustrated by Color Photography*, V. III, No. 6, by Nature Study Publishing, Chicago, 1898.

"Cadillac," by Jörg Buntrock.

"Human Heart Diagram," from *Outlines of Human Physiology* by George Hayward, 1834.

"Camera Obscura Box, 18th Century," unknown illustrator.

"Horse Bones," unknown illustrator, from *Nordisk familjebok*, 1876–1899.

"Full Moon," courtesy of NASA.

Grateful acknowledgement is made to the editors of the following publications where some of these poems, some of which have been revised, first appeared:

Sixfold (2015, 2016): "Behind the Glass," "Two Young Wives," "Housewife," "She Learns How to Disappear," "Aerie," "Elegy for a Body," and "I Think My Taste Is Questionable."

Our Space: Shorts & Poetry from the Houston Community (2015): "Morning Song."

Literary Orphans (Issue 26, 2016): "Peony Red."

Dreamlike Art and Deviation by John Bernhard (2018): "Anvil Crawler."

I am beyond grateful to the folks at Finishing Line Press for believing in these poems. Much love and gratitude to my writing community, my extended Writespace family, and writers Cassandra Rose Clarke, Chloe N. Clark, Lois Stark, Michael Glazner, Tony Clavelli, Eloísa Pérez-Lozano, Kate Lechler, Bonnie Jo Stufflebeam, Shannon Connor Winward, Maggie Rose Berardo, and Jody T. Morse. Thank you all for your proofreading, guidance and moral support, for being my cheering section.

About the Cover Artist

Geoff Gallice is an entomologist based in the Peruvian Amazon. His research focuses on the ecology, evolution, and conservation of butterflies in South America, with an emphasis on the clearwing butterflies. He is particularly interested in what causes some butterflies to be common yet others rare, and what this means for the long term survival of species in a changing world. Geoff is also active in applied conservation, and leads a non-profit—the Alliance for a Sustainable Amazon—that is working to conserve biodiversity and other natural resources in southeastern Peru. Learn more about Geoff's work in Peru at www.sustainableamazon.org.

About the Author

Holly Lyn Walrath received her Master's degree in Creative Writing from the University of Denver. Her short fiction and poetry has appeared in *Strange Horizons, Fireside Fiction, Liminality, Crab Fat Magazine, Mithila Review, Nonbinary Review,* and other places. She works as a freelance editor and currently resides in Seabrook, Texas, just five minutes from NASA Johnson Space Center. She has two cats named Cleo and Panda and a husband who is a pediatric physical therapist. Along with writing, she enjoys geekery, books, self-aggrandizing statements, feminism, dystopia, and cat pictures.

Follow her on Twitter @HollyLynWalrath or visit her website at www.hlwalrath.com.